W9-BRC-970

WITHDRAWN

WITHDRAWN

ANIMAL SCAVENGERS

Hyenas

SANDRA MARKLE

⌐ LERNER PUBLICATIONS COMPANY / MINNEAPOLIS

THE ANIMAL WORLD IS FULL OF SCAVENGERS.

Scavengers are the cleanup crew who find and eat carrion (dead animals) in order to survive. Every day, animals are born and animals die. Without scavengers, the bodies of dead animals would rot away slowly. The decaying flesh would smell bad and take up space. It could also pollute water and attract flies and other disease-carrying insects. Fortunately, scavengers everywhere eat dead and dying animals before they have time to rot. In the grasslands and dry deserts of Africa, hyenas are part of the scavenger cleanup crew. Spotted hyenas are just as likely to kill their own prey. *But brown hyenas count on carrion for their main food supply.*

It's late afternoon in the Kalahari Desert of southern Africa. The rainy season has started. The migrating herds of springbok, hartebeest, and gemsbok have returned to share the grass with the wildebeest and other full-time residents. Predators, such as lions and cheetahs, have followed the grazing herds, hunting where the prey is plentiful. More food for the hunters also means more leftovers for the scavengers, such as the brown hyena.

A female brown hyena wakes from her daylong rest in the shade. She yawns, stretching her big jaws. She looks something like a shaggy German shepherd. She is the same size, with similar dark brown and black coloring, a square muzzle, and pointed ears. But her jaws are much more powerful than those of a dog. She also has bigger, stronger teeth, which can easily crush bones. When a hyena scavenges carrion, it eats everything, including the bones.

As the sun sinks lower in the sky and the temperature drops a little, the brown hyena goes to visit the nearby communal (group) den. Brown hyenas are social animals. They live with a clan, a group of brown hyenas that recognize each other, share a home territory, and raise cubs together. During the rainy season, food is abundant and some adult males join the clan. The female lifts her tail as she greets her clan members. Then she heads out in search of a meal. Hyenas forage alone.

The hyena's pace is about the same speed as human jogging. She stops frequently, though, to squat and leave a scent marking with her urine. This way, the female brown hyena lets her clan members know she passed this spot. It's also a warning to brown hyenas from other clans that this territory is claimed.

In the rainy season, it's easier to find water. For eight months, rain had not fallen on the Kalahari. Lakes and rivers dried up. During that time, the brown hyena got some of her water by eating juicy fruits, such as tsamma melons. These round green melons are about half the size of a soccer ball. Even now she stops to munch a melon when she finds one.

Nearby, a pair of spotted hyenas charges a herd of wildebeest to start them running.

When a wildebeest calf lags behind the others, the spotted hyenas focus on it. A third spotted hyena joins in the chase. Spotted hyenas can run as fast as 35 miles (about 55 kilometers) per hour. They keep after the wildebeest calf until it tires and slows enough for them to catch it. A jackal circles, waiting for an opportunity to rush in and steal a bite.

The spotted hyenas only have time to gulp down a few mouthfuls before the lions attack them. Lions are larger and more than twice as heavy as spotted hyenas. Two hyenas immediately give up and run away. One stays to fight, but the lions drive it off too.

The female brown hyena, who has been watching the hunt, sees the lions settle down to eat. The lions will eat only the juiciest parts of the wildebeest and leave the rest. The saliva rises in the brown hyena's mouth. She is hungry for the parts these hunters will leave. But as eager as she is for a mouthful of the fresh meat, she doesn't wait. It could take hours for the lions to finish. So the female brown hyena continues her search for a meal somewhere else.

As the day slips into night, moonlight paints the Kalahari with soft, silver light and shadows. The female brown hyena can see well in this dim light. But she depends mainly on her keen sense of smell when foraging in the dark. She can detect the strong odor of rotting carrion from a long way off.

This night, she follows her nose to the remains of a giraffe that lions killed the day before. She digs in, ripping off any remaining bits of flesh. Then she cracks open the giraffe's bones and licks out the fatty marrow. She eats the hard bone too. Hyenas have strong jaws and teeth. They also have unusually strong acid in their stomachs. The acid helps them to digest almost every part of an animal, including bones.

When there's plenty of food, a brown hyena eats about 5.5 to 6 pounds (about 2.5 to 3 kilograms) a day. But the female may not find carrion every day. So when she's full, the female hyena carries away a leftover piece to store for later.

Adult brown hyenas have such strong jaws that they can carry loads that weigh as much as 17 pounds (about 8 kg) in their mouths. They are able to carry these loads long distances across rough ground. This female hauls her leftover piece for nearly 1 mile (more than 1 km) before pushing it under a bush.

The female hyena doesn't go back to claim her stored food the next evening. About three months ago, she mated with a male that briefly joined her clan. A cub has been growing inside her body and is ready to be born. When she returns to her clan's communal den at dawn, she looks for the abandoned aardvark burrow that's nearby. Crawling just inside the opening, the hyena gives birth to the newest member of the clan, another little female. At birth, the cub isn't much longer than a soft drink can. Her eyes are closed. They will open in about a week. In two more weeks, she will come out of her birth den to nurse while her mother naps between foraging trips.

Soon the cub is big enough to come out of the den to explore when her mother goes hunting. But the little female stays close enough to scoot back inside if a predator, such as a spotted hyena or a lion, is nearby. On her own, the cub has dug a tunnel inside her birth den. It has an opening just big enough for her. If a predator pursues her to her den, she crawls into her special tunnel. Hungry predators can't reach her there.

When the cub is about three months old, her mother carries her to the communal den. There, the little female joins the other cubs already living there. Since hyenas may give birth at any time of the year, some of the cubs at the den are older and bigger than she is. From now on, though, she'll stay with them and play with them. More important, any of the clan's mothers will let her nurse. Brown hyena cubs continue to nurse until they are about fifteen months old. Being able to nurse from any of the clan's nursing females means that the little female will survive even if her own mother dies.

One night, the female brown hyena fails to find anything to eat. So she keeps on searching instead of heading home to nurse her cub. She knows her cub will be safe with the other females in the den. When her sensitive nose picks up the scent of lionesses, she stays on their track. The brown hyena hears the lionesses eating before she sees them. Since she's had no luck finding food that night, she settles down to wait for the lionesses to leave. She waits through the rest of the night. At last, when the day is bright and hot, the lionesses go in search of a shady spot to sleep. Finally, the female brown hyena is able to claim the remains of the gemsbok for herself.

As the female cub gets older, she explores on her own and with the other cubs. This way, she begins to learn her territory. But she always goes back to the clan's communal den when the adults return. At least one of the adults is likely to bring home something for the cubs to eat. Eating solid food helps the youngsters to grow bigger. It also helps the cubs learn the smell and taste of the foods they'll be searching for as adults. Gnawing and chewing this food helps the cubs develop the strong jaw muscles they'll need to crunch bones. Bones are often the only part of a carcass left for these scavengers.

The young female searches for food alone, though she is less likely to find it than the adults. More and more often, though, she is able to feed herself. The rains are over, and the time of drought is coming to the Kalahari. Water is scarce and plants are drying up. Many of the predators have left the desert, so there are fewer scraps for scavengers to eat. On the other hand, the weakest members of the herds that stay in the desert will die. Their carcasses provide food for scavengers.

One night, the young brown hyena follows her nose to a dead gemsbok. She finds several members of her clan already there. If there had been less to eat, the hyenas would have taken turns. The first to arrive would have eaten first. But there is so much meat that they all eat together.

Another night, the young female is lucky. She finds a food treasure—an abandoned ostrich nest full of eggs. Each ostrich egg is equal to about twenty-four chicken eggs, so the nest contains a feast.

The little female has never eaten an egg before. She watches an adult brown hyena break open the top of the eggshell, lap out the gooey contents with her tongue, and chomp down on the shell. The little hyena eats an egg the same way. Her stomach acid will break down the hard shell.

With plenty to eat, the young female continues to grow bigger and stronger. One late afternoon, she learns one of the most important lessons of all—to stay away from feeding predators. Following the scent of fresh blood, she comes too close to feeding lions.

One of the lions charges her, and she runs off as fast as she can. Other young brown hyenas aren't that lucky. With the clan's help, most of the brown hyena cubs survive to become young adults. But many young adults don't live past their first year on their own.

The young female brown hyena is one of the survivors. By the time she is nearly three years old, she's full grown. She's even big and strong enough to sometimes take prey away from a predator, such as a cheetah. This cat is about the same size as the brown hyena. It runs away rather than risk a leg to the brown hyena's bone-crushing bite.

The young hyena spends most days resting in a shady spot at the clan's communal den site. Sometimes, though, she stays away foraging for several days looking for food.

When she finds a meaty meal, she eats her fill and then carries a chunk back to the den. A week before, one of the clan's females brought two fuzzy cubs to the communal den. Now it's the young female's turn to help the clan raise its newest members.

And soon, she will give birth to the cub developing inside her. With the birth of new cubs, the brown hyena clan and the Kalahari's cleanup crew of scavengers will be another generation stronger.

Looking Back

- Look back through the book at the pictures of brown hyenas. How are they like the spotted hyenas on pages 9, 10, and 11? How are they different from spotted hyenas?

- Check how the brown hyenas' eyes appear to glow on page 28. That glow is actually light reflecting off a mirrorlike layer at the back of the eye. This layer bounces light to light-sensing cells in the eye, helping brown hyenas see in dim light.

- Look closely at the brown hyena eating an egg on page 31. Notice that she doesn't crack the egg wide open. Instead, the brown hyena carefully bites a hole in the top of the egg. That keeps the gooey contents from spilling and absorbing into the ground.

Glossary

CARRION: a dead animal that a scavenger eats

CLAN: a group of hyenas that recognize one another and share a territory

CUB: a young hyena

DEN: a protected place for giving birth, sleeping, and eating. The female hyena uses a burrow as a birth den for her cubs. The clan shares a communal den site too.

DIGESTION: the process of eating and the breakdown of food in the body for energy

HERDS: groups of the same kind of animals that feed and travel together

MARROW: the soft, fatty material that fills the central cavity of bones

PREDATOR: an animal that hunts and eats other animals to survive

PREY: an animal that a predator catches to eat

SCAVENGERS: animals that feed on dead animals

SCENT: an animal's sense of smell or an odor left behind by an animal

TERRITORY: the area within which the clan usually searches for food

Further Information

BOOKS

Hopf, Alice Lightner. *Hyenas.* New York: Putnam, 1983. This books offers an introduction to the life and traits of the hyena.

Morgan, Sally. *Hyenas.* Chicago: Raintree/Steck-Vaughn, 2003. This is a book at all of the hyenas of Africa, including the spotted hyena and the brown hyena.

Stone, Lynn M. *Hyenas.* Rourke, 1990. This book describes where and how hyenas live in Africa.

VIDEOS

Families in the Wild Hyenas (Goldhil Home Media 2, 2001). Discover insights about hyenas, experts of the suprise attack. See hyena clan life in action.

National Geographic's Eternal Enemies: Lions and Hyenas (National Geographic, 1992). This film dramatically brings to life the competition for prey between lions and hyenas. The hyenas steal prey from the lions, and the lions attack and kill hyenas.

WEBSITES

Predator Conservation Trust. *Brown Hyena Information.* http://www.predatorconservation.com/brown%20hyena .htm. Learn more about brown hyenas, including what they eat, how they act, and how they sound.

Index

With love for the children of Hillview Academy in Christchurch, New Zealand

The author would like to thank Dr. Christine Drea, assistant professor of biological anthropology and anatomy at Duke University and collaborator on the UC-Berkeley Hyena Project; Dr. Gus Mills, research fellow with SAN Parks and head of the Carnivore Conservation Group of the Endangered Wildlife Trust; and Ingrid Wiesel, researcher with the Brown Hyena Research Project, Namibia, for sharing their expertise and enthusiasm. The author would also like to express a special thank-you to Skip Jeffery for his help and support through the creative process.

Photo Acknowledgments

The images in this book are used with the permission of: © Martin Harvey/ Gallo Images/ CORBIS, pp. 1, 36; © Peter Johnson/ CORBIS, pp. 3, 15, 33; © Mitsuaki Iwago/ Minden Pictures, pp. 4, 9, 10, 11; © Dave Hamman, pp. 5, 8, 23, 27, 31, 35; © Martin Harvey/ Peter Arnold, Inc., p. 6; © Anthony Bannister/ Gallo Images/ CORBIS, p. 13; © Frantisek Staud/ www.phototravels.net, p. 14; © Gus Mills, pp. 17, 19, 24, 28; © Thys Van der Merwe, pp. 20, 37; © Roger De La Harpe/ Gallo Images/ CORBIS, p. 32. Front cover: © Richard du Toit/ naturepl.com. Back cover (top): ©David Hamman/ Animals Animals/ Earth Scenes. Back cover (bottom): *Army Ants:* © Christian Ziegler; *Hyenas:* © Richard du Toit/ naturepl.com; *Jackals:* © Beverly Joubert/ National Geographic/ Getty Images; *Tasmanian Devils:* Photodisc Royalty Free by Getty Images; *Vultures:* © Chris Hellier/ CORBIS; *Wolverines:* © Daniel J. Cox/ naturalexposures.com.

Copyright © 2005 by Sandra Markle

All rights reserved. International copyright secured. No part of this book may be reproduced, stored in a retrieval system, or transmitted in any form or by any means—electronic, mechanical, photocopying, recording, or otherwise—without the prior written permission of Lerner Publications Company, except for brief quotations in an acknowledged review.

Lerner Publications Company
A division of Lerner Publishing Group
241 First Avenue North
Minneapolis, MN 55401

Website address: www.lernerbooks.com

Library of Congress Cataloging-in-Publication Data

Markle, Sandra.
    Hyenas / by Sandra Markle.
      p.   cm. — (Animal scavengers)
    Includes bibliographical references and index.
    ISBN-13: 978–0–8225–3194–4 (lib. bdg. : alk. paper)
    ISBN-10: 0–8225–3194–1 (lib. bdg. : alk. paper)
    1. Hyenas—Juvenile literature. I. Title. II. Series: Markle, Sandra. Animal scavengers.
QL737.C24M27 2005
599.74'3—dc22   2004029659

Manufactured in the United States of America
1 2 3 4 5 6 – DP – 10 09 08 07 06 05

READ ANIMAL PREDATORS,
A BOOKLIST TOP 10 YOUTH
NONFICTION SERIES
BY SANDRA MARKLE

Crocodiles
Great White Sharks
Killer Whales
Lions
Owls
Polar Bears
Wolves